Children of the World

South Africa

To Tumi and her generation of all races as they grow up in the new South Africa.

For a free color catalog describing Gareth Stevens' list of high quality children's books, call 1-800-341-3569 (USA) or 1-800-461-9120 (Canada).

For their help in the preparation of *Children of the World: South Africa*, the editors gratefully thank the Milwaukee Public Library; the International Institute of Wisconsin, Milwaukee; and Peter Kwele. The authors thank Peter Celliers of Ellis Associates in New York; Jimmy Ntintile of Face to Face Tours in Johannesburg; Bettie Wessels of SATOUR in Johannesburg; and South African Airways, each of whom assisted us in ways far beyond our travel arrangements.

Flag illustration on page 48, © Flag Research Center.

Library of Congress Cataloging-in-Publication Data

Rogers, Barbara Radcliffe.
    South Africa / photography by Stillman Rogers; written by Barbara Radcliffe Rogers.
        p. cm. — (Children of the world)
    Includes bibliographical references and index.
    Summary: Presents the life of a twelve-year-old girl who lives in Soweto, a suburb of Johannesburg, under a system of apartheid. There is a reference section of information about South Africa.
    ISBN 0-8368-0247-0
    1. South Africa—Juvenile literature. 2. Children—South Africa—Juvenile literature. 3. Children, Black—South Africa—Juvenile literature. [1. South Africa—Social life and customs.]
I. Rogers, Stillman, 1939-   ill.   II. Title. III. Series.
IV. Series: Children of the world (Milwaukee, Wis.)
DT1721.R64   1990   89-43188

A Gareth Stevens Children's Books edition
Edited, designed, and produced by

Gareth Stevens Children's Books
1555 North RiverCenter Drive, Suite 201
Milwaukee, WI 53212, USA

Series editors: Valerie Weber and Mark Sachner
Editor: Kelli Peduzzi
Research editor: John D. Rateliff
Designer: Sabine Huschke
Map design: Sheri Gibbs

Printed in the United States of America

  2 3 4 5 6 7 8 9 97 96 95 94 93 92 91

Children of the World
South Africa

Text by Barbara Radcliffe Rogers
Photographs by Stillman Rogers

Gareth Stevens Children's Books
MILWAUKEE

. . . a note about *Children of the World*:

The children of the world live in fishing towns and urban centers, on islands and in mountain valleys, on sheep ranches and fruit farms. This series follows one child in each country through the pattern of his or her life. Candid photographs show the children with their families, at school, at play, and in their communities. The text describes the dreams of the children and, often through their own words, tells how they see themselves and their lives.

Each book also explores events that are unique to the country in which the child lives, including festivals, religious ceremonies, and national holidays. The *Children of the World* series does more than tell about foreign countries. It introduces the children of each country and shows readers what it is like to be a child in that country.

Children of the World includes the following published and soon-to-be-published titles:

Australia	El Salvador	Japan	Spain
Belize	England	Jordan	Sweden
Bhutan	Finland	Malaysia	Tanzania
Bolivia	France	Mexico	Thailand
Brazil	Greece	Nepal	Turkey
Burkina Faso	Guatemala	New Zealand	USSR
Burma (Myanmar)	Honduras	Nicaragua	Vietnam
Canada	Hong Kong	Panama	West Germany
China	Hungary	Philippines	Yugoslavia
Costa Rica	India	Poland	Zambia
Cuba	Indonesia	Singapore	
Czechoslovakia	Ireland	South Africa	
Egypt	Italy	South Korea	

... and about *South Africa*:

Tumi Motube is a 12-year-old girl from Soweto, an area outside of Johannesburg, where she and her mother live in one small room. Tumi, a black girl, lives under the system of apartheid, or separation of the races according to skin color. She helps her mother with household chores, does the marketing, and cooks special dishes.

To enhance this book's value in libraries and classrooms, comprehensive reference sections include up-to-date information about South African geography, demographics, language, currency, education, culture, industry, and natural resources. *South Africa* also features a bibliography, research topics, activity projects, and discussions of such subjects as its three capital cities, its history, languages, political system, and ethnic and religious composition.

The living conditions and experiences of children in South Africa vary according to economic, environmental, and ethnic circumstances. The reference sections help bring to life for young readers the diversity and richness of the culture and heritage of South Africa. Of particular interest are discussions of South Africa's tribal history, natural resources, government, and its long and exciting history.

CONTENTS

Tumi Motube and her mother, Elizabeth, relax together in their yard.

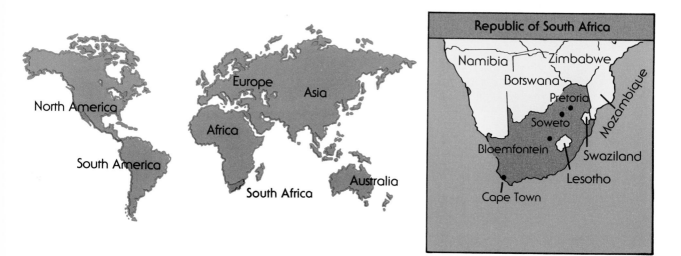

North America

South America

Europe

Asia

Africa

South Africa

Australia

Republic of South Africa

Namibia

Zimbabwe

Botswana

Mozambique

Pretoria

Soweto

Bloemfontein

Swaziland

Lesotho

Cape Town

LIVING IN SOUTH AFRICA:
Tumi, a Girl from Soweto

Tumi Motube is a 12-year-old girl from the Republic of South Africa, a country at the very tip of the African continent. Tumi lives in Soweto, an area just outside of Johannesburg, her country's largest city.

Tumi's real first name is Euginia, but her parents also gave her the name of Boitumelo (pronounced boy-TOO-meh-low). In the Tswana language, the name means "happiness." Maybe this is why Tumi is always smiling. Her family, friends, and teachers all call her Tumi, the nickname for Boitumelo.

Unlike most Soweto children, who usually come from homes filled with brothers and sisters, Tumi is an only child. Her parents are divorced and she lives with her mother, Elizabeth Motube. Tumi never sees her father.

Boitumelo, Tumi's full name, means "happiness" in her native Tswana language.

Living in Soweto

"Soweto" (pronounced so-WEH-toe) sounds like an African word, but it is really made up of the first letters of SOuth WEstern TOwnships. Soweto includes 33 townships where only black South Africans may live. Although 74% of South Africa's people are black and only 14% are white, blacks do not have the same rights as whites. Being black, Tumi and her mother must live in the black or Coloured townships, integrated neighborhoods, or in regions called homelands, many of which are poor, rural areas.

The system that tells Tumi and other black South Africans where they may live is called "apartheid." In the Afrikaans language, this means "separateness," and the law separates people according to their skin color. The government has begun to relax the laws of apartheid that have for decades separated blacks and whites on buses, in restaurants, and even in movie theaters. But Tumi and her mother still may not live wherever they like.

In poorer Soweto neighborhoods, people fence their yards with whatever they can find. ▶
Inset: Graffiti on a Soweto wall protests apartheid.
Below: Shacks that homeowners rent out to others often share one water source.

Tumi's home is very small, with only one room. Although it's tiny, it is in a wealthy neighborhood of Soweto, attached to the back of a lovely brick house that is surrounded by a lawn and rose gardens. Tumi's home was designed as a maid's room, but the people who own the house were not using it, so they rented it to Tumi's mother. Nearby lives Nelson Mandela, a leader for black rights in South Africa. But not all neighborhoods in Soweto are as fine as this one.

In the back yards of the poorer parts of Soweto, people have built separate little one-room buildings with tin roofs. They build these for their married children to live in, and as more children grow up, they build more of them. On some small house lots, 15 or 20 of these separate little buildings crowd together. They all share one bathroom and water supply with the original house. Whole neighborhoods of homes have become "shanty towns" with the addition of these little buildings.

As in villages throughout other parts of Africa, people spend most of their day outdoors. ▶
Below: The new home of the family of Nelson Mandela, the leader of the African National Congress, in a well-to-do section of Soweto.

Other areas in Soweto have become shanty towns in another way. Many people who come to the city looking for jobs have no place to live and no money, so they camp out in public parks and soccer fields. They make shelters out of whatever wood or tin they can find, or from dried mud and grass. These people are called squatters.

The government does not like to have people living in such poor shelters, but it can't build enough public housing for the squatters. Many times, the government has moved people out of the shanties and bull-dozed the areas, but new shanty towns spring up to replace them. People who are returned by the government to their villages or to rural tribal "homelands" often move back to build new shanties in the same cities. Whenever Tumi and her mother pass one of the shanty towns, they think how lucky they were to find one nice room in overcrowded Soweto.

A typical shanty town near Johannesburg. Metal roofing is a common and inexpensive building material for shanty homes.
Inset: Children attend nursery school in a shanty village.

Because she must live in Soweto, Tumi's mother, Elizabeth, does not live near the hairdressers' shop where she works. She has to travel more than an hour on the bus each morning to get there.

Until four years ago, Elizabeth and Tumi lived in Kimberley with Tumi's grandparents. In Kimberly, Elizabeth's work was even farther from their home, so she moved to Soweto to find work in the big city. At first, Tumi stayed in Kimberley with her grandparents. But both Tumi and her mother were lonely for each other, so they decided that Tumi would move, too. At first, it was hard for Tumi to start in a new school, but it was worth it to live with her mother again.

Tumi and Elizabeth enjoy doing things together when Tumi is not in school and her mother is not working at the hairdressers'. They cook dinner on Sundays and Wednesdays, Elizabeth's days off. Sometimes they visit their friends, Jimmy and Ophelia Ntintile and their son, Leboni.

Tumi's mother has ten days of vacation every year, which she takes during Tumi's school vacations in December and April. Then they travel by train to Kimberley to visit Tumi's grandparents.

Tumi often has dinner ready by the time her mother returns home from work. ▶

Soweto has homes on every economic level, from shanties to very fine houses.

At Home with Tumi

Tumi and Elizabeth's bed takes up most of their one room and is covered with a bright red and white plaid bedspread. Tumi's mother has put large red pillows against the wall. They lean against these pillows to use the bed as a couch. This makes a comfortable place where Tumi studies in the evening.

Along the walls are three chairs, a bureau, and a tiny table with an electric hot plate on which they cook their meals. Afterward, Tumi washes the dishes in the bathroom sink. Because the weather in Soweto is usually warm and pleasant, Tumi and her mother spend a lot of time out of doors. The landlord does not often allow Tumi to play in the big yard behind the house, but she and her mother may use the small yard in front of their door.

Tumi tells her mother about her day.

Ready for bed, with night cream on her face, Tumi studies for a little while longer.

In the Morning

Tumi wakes up at 6:00 a.m. to have breakfast with her mother before Elizabeth begins her long bus ride to work. Tumi's favorite breakfast is a bowl of Kellogg's bran flakes. After her mother leaves, Tumi tidies up the house and does other chores. She washes clothes or listens to rock music on Radio 5 while she irons. Then she packs her books and lunch into her canvas school bag.

Tumi has to leave the house by 7:30 a.m. to walk to school, but she goes earlier if she has finished her work. She hurries so she will have time to play with her friends Lerato, Girly, Daena, and Sindi. They play jump rope or dodge ball until school begins. Since the boys are usually playing with the soccer balls, Tumi and her friends use a tennis ball for dodgeball.

Top inset: Getting ready for the school day, Tumi irons her white school uniform blouse.
Bottom inset: Tumi carries her books and lunch to school in a canvas bag.
During a lively game of dodgeball, Tumi's schoolmates watch as she tries to duck away from the ball. ▶

Boepakitso School

Tumi goes to Boepakitso School, a public school several blocks from her home. In the Tswana language, Boepakitso means "digging for knowledge."

At 8:00 a.m., when the bell rings, all the students from preschool through standard (grade) five gather in the courtyard between the three buildings and say a Christian prayer together. Then Tumi goes to her classroom. Some of Tumi's classmates are older than she is and some are younger. Because South Africa has no set age when children must begin school, and because parents sometimes need older children to stay home and look after younger siblings, children start school at different ages.

The students of Boepakitso School have planted a garden around the school sign. ▶
Below: The Boepakitso School is in a new, modern building.

Mr. Leteate carefully explains the parts of a leaf to Tumi's class.

The classroom is a lively place where Tumi's teachers, Mr. Leteate and Mr. Mbuyisa, make learning interesting. They ask many questions to see if the children understand what they have read in their books, and Tumi raises her hand when she knows the answer. Discussion is lively, and Tumi's friends are all eager to show that they have been studying hard by taking part in class. Sometimes Mr. Leteate says funny things to help the students remember what they are learning.

Tumi's teachers speak English in the classroom, except when they are teaching Afrikaans or Tswana. All over South Africa, both black and white children learn English, Afrikaans, and the most common language of the native peoples of their area. In Tumi's school, this language is Tswana, spoken by the black people of the Transvaal, the region around Johannesburg. Tumi's favorite subject in school is Afrikaans, the language of the white Dutch settlers of South Africa, who are known as Afrikaners. Along with languages, Tumi and her classmates study mathematics, science, geography, health, religion, and history.

Late in the morning, the students have a recess and eat their lunches. Those who live nearby can go home, but Tumi and her friends take their lunches to school. Tumi's lunch is a sandwich, which she carries in a square plastic box. Some students have "carry money" and can go to the little shops near school to buy hot food. The school has no lunch program or lunchroom, so the children go outside to eat, where they can be as noisy as they want.

Tumi brings home her school books each night so she can do her homework.

After lunch, Tumi and her friends play in the school yard or sing and do a dance with steps similar to the American square dance. Sometimes the younger children join in and get underfoot, and the dance ends with everyone mixed up and laughing. When the bell rings again, everyone returns to their classrooms until 2:00 p.m., when classes end with a short prayer.

Tumi and her friends sing and dance together during recess.

Many of the students live in typical South African homes, where several children share a tiny space with mothers, grandmothers, and grown-up sisters and their children. (Black fathers in South Africa often work far from home because they must go where the jobs are.) In such a crowd, it's usually impossible to find a quiet place to study, so the schools remain open until 5:00 p.m. for children to stay and do their homework. The teachers also stay to help with work the children do not understand. This is especially helpful to those children whose parents do not speak English or Afrikaans and are not able to help them with their homework.

In social studies class, Tumi is learning how governments work.

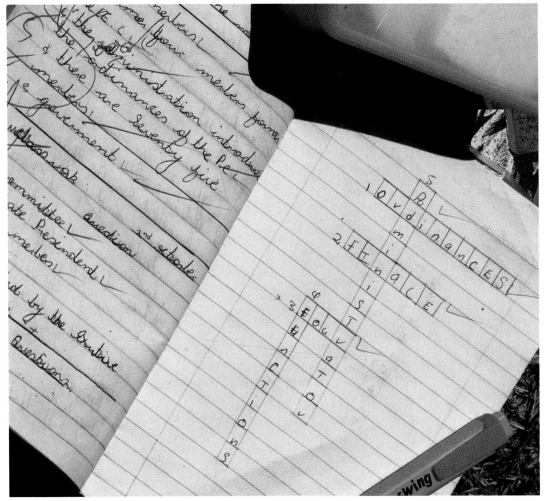

Tumi and her teacher talk about the news articles that they are putting on the bulletin board.

Sometimes Tumi stays to talk to Mr. Leteate and Mr. Mbuyisa, or to help them design the bulletin board in the back of the classroom. They put up news articles of current events to stay informed because many families do not get newspapers.

27

After-school Shopping

If Tumi has "carry money" and is not going grocery shopping later, she stops at the food shop near school. She selects a crispy, hot piece of fried bread dough or a little bag of French fries to eat as she walks home. Since most of her friends go in different directions, she walks alone. Once Tumi reaches home, she changes out of her school uniform and begins her homework. On nice days, she studies out of doors.

French fries and fried bread are two of Tumi's favorite after-school snacks.

Tumi has learned from her mother how to be a smart shopper at the grocery store.

Because Tumi's mother does not get home from work until 7:00 p.m., Tumi is responsible for shopping and starting their dinner. When her mother has asked her to buy food, she walks for 45 minutes to the Blackchain Supermarket, a large grocery store in a Soweto shopping mall. She has learned from her mother how to choose good, fresh vegetables and to compare prices when she shops. In such a small house, they cannot store very much food, so Tumi buys only enough to last one or two days.

The shopping center is an exciting place, even if Tumi is only there to buy groceries. It is noisy and busy with people and full of the smells of fried chicken and hamburgers. Tumi enjoys window shopping at the sports shop and especially likes to look at the new styles in the Benetton window.

The shopping mall is two stories tall and built around an open courtyard, with walkways much like the ones at Tumi's school. Several fast-food shops, with tables and chairs, are set up in the sunny courtyard. Before she leaves the mall, Tumi sometimes buys ice cream from one of these shops.

Tumi's mother gave her extra money to buy ice cream — a special treat — for the walk home from the mall.

Window shopping is one of Tumi's favorite activities. She wonders if the skirt in the window would look good on her.

The Lure of the Marketplace

Not all of Soweto's stores are in shopping centers. As in most other countries in Africa, many vendors in Soweto are outside on the street, selling fresh oranges and apples, clothing, candy, meats, and cooked foods. Since small homes like Tumi's usually don't have ovens, many people buy meat already cooked. The smell of these meats sizzling on open *brais*, or grills, makes Tumi hungry.

On one street, Tumi passes stalls filled with strange-looking roots and barks and plants of the herbal healers, or *dinkatas*. They are not "witch doctors" casting spells, but people who have learned about medicinal herbs from their parents and grandparents, who were also dinkatas. They know which plants will sooth a sore throat or help a cut heal faster.

Farmers sell their produce at markets like these all over South Africa.
Inset: A *dinkata* sells herbs and plants used in traditional medicine.

The many stands set up along the streets in Soweto are handy, but their prices are high. Instead of buying at the street stalls, Tumi and her mother do most of their shopping at the Blackchain, where prices are lower.

Where many food sellers have gathered in one place, busy markets have formed. Each of the stands is really a tiny store for one kind of product. Some are filled with mounds of red-hot spices, some with fresh fish from the Indian Ocean, some with all the spices that go into curry powder, and some with fresh, plucked chickens or meats.

The market people represent all the different cultures of South Africa, too. In one of these markets, Tumi may see a Shangan lady with blankets wrapped around her to make her look fat, or a tiny Malay lady wrapped in a brightly colored silk *sari*. The markets are noisy with many languages, as everyone talks at once, and friends call from one stall to the next.

Above: Colorful and fragrant spices and foods fill the Indian market stalls.
Below: Hot peppers are common in both Indian and African foods.
Colorful flowers, like the ones in this Cape Town market, are sold all over the world. ▶

The Food Tumi Eats

The foods that Tumi and her mother eat are influenced by their own Tswana heritage, and also by the many different peoples that make up South Africa. Curried dishes, for example, are enjoyed by blacks and whites, as well as by the Indian immigrants who introduced the exotic mix of spices to South Africa.

Many traditional African dishes are cooked in one pot, a way of cooking that originated over village campfires long ago to save fuel. It is still a handy method for families like Tumi's, which have only a hot plate to cook dinner on. The tasty stews that Tumi's mother makes are a combination of meats and vegetables simmered together. Elizabeth also fries sweet potatoes by mashing them with an egg and a little flour and dropping them by the spoonful into hot fat.

Tumi's favorite food is steak cooked over an open fire on a brai. The meat is juicy and tastes like the woodsmoke from the fire. Her mother usually cooks ribs and other meats on the brai, but they have steak on special occasions, such as Tumi's birthday.

The brai is Tumi's favorite way to cook meat. The wood gives the food a special flavor.

Above: Elizabeth has cooked *babootie*, a dish made of ground meat seasoned with bay leaves.
Below: Spicy side dishes, such as these chutneys and pickles, accompany an Indian meal.

Tumi's Special Dish

An easy dish that Tumi cooks often is yellow rice, and she has it ready when her mother arrives home from work. Here is the recipe for Tumi's rice dish. It is popular all over South Africa, but it uses ingredients that are easy to find anywhere. It is cooked on a hot stove, so be sure to have an adult present before you begin.

Yellow Rice

2 cups (500 ml) of boiling water in a large saucepan
1 cup (250 ml) of rice
1 stick of cinnamon
1/2 teaspoon (2.5 ml) of tumeric
1 teaspoon (5 ml) of salt
1 teaspoon (5 ml) of sugar (South Africans use much more.)
1 tablespoon (15 ml) of butter
1/2 cup (125 ml) of raisins

Rice and a spice called tumeric are the main ingredients in Yellow Rice.

Add all the ingredients, except the raisins, to the boiling water. Cover the pot and cook over very low heat for about 20 minutes. Test the rice to see if it's done. Be careful to let it cool first so it won't burn your tongue. When it is tender, but not mushy, stir in the raisins and turn off the heat. Let the pot sit, covered, for five to ten minutes until the raisins are plump. This recipe serves two to four people.

As it cooks, the rice turns a bright yellow.

A Birthday Trip to Johannesburg

It's October 8th, Tumi's birthday, a day she has been eagerly looking forward to for weeks. Her mother has promised to take her to downtown Johannesburg to buy new tennis shoes. Elizabeth has the day off from work, so their neighbor, Jimmy Ntintile, picks Tumi up at school in his car and drives them to the center of the city. This is a treat, because it would take them a long time to get there on the bus.

They go to a brand new sports shop filled with all kinds of sporting equipment. Pictures of South African sports stars and of its famous rugby team, the Springboks, line the walls. The man in the store helps Tumi try on every pair of shoes in her size until she finds just the pair she wants.

When Tumi leaves the store with her new shoes, she thinks that this has already been a perfect day, but Jimmy has another treat for her. On their way home, they stop at Gold Reef City, a restored town from Johannesburg's gold rush days, where Tumi rides an old locomotive.

The clerk in the sports shop patiently helps Tumi choose her new tennis shoes. ▶
Below: Gold Reef City is a place where tourists can see how Johannesburg looked in its frontier days, over a century ago.

Cape Town, a city at the very tip of the African continent, sits at the foot of flat Table Mountain.
Inset: The Drakensberg, or Dragon's Mountain, is a tall mountain range southeast of Johannesburg.
The section shown here is called the Drei Rondavel, which means "three houses."

The Many Faces of South Africa

Tumi and many other black South African children have grown up in cities, far from the villages of their ancestors. They no longer hear and see the stories of their people acted out by dancers dressed in bright-colored beads or hear them told in song, as they are in village celebrations. This oral tradition is how the history of many of Africa's peoples has been passed down from one generation to the next. Many black families in the cities worry that their children will grow up without the cultural roots enjoyed by village children.

Near Johannesburg, an entire Zulu village, or *kraal*, has moved from its worn-out farm lands and started over again. On Sundays, the villagers welcome visitors to see their celebrations and dancing.

Each Sunday, the kraal at Heia Ranch is filled with black families, and some whites as well, who bring their children to enjoy a brai and see the village. Many families come again and again, so that the stories and history will become a part of their children's lives.

Many of the peoples of South Africa do intricate beadwork. ▶
Below: Zulus perform dances that tell about events in their history.

44

Most of the children who go to school with Tumi are Tswana, a people who live in the northern part of South Africa. But they are only one of the many peoples living in Soweto and throughout the rest of South Africa.

Among the other native South African peoples, the Zulu are the most numerous, and Zulu is the language most often heard in Soweto. The Xhosa, the Ndebele, the Sotho, and others make up the rest of the black population. Non-black South Africans include Malays, Indians, Afrikaners, and people of British origin.

Wherever one goes in South Africa, one sees people of different racial and tribal groups and hears their different languages. It is said that South Africans speak more slowly than most other people because they are so accustomed to talking to people whose language is different from their own.

Although growing up in a country with such great differences will often be difficult for Tumi, it is also exciting. She is living in an especially fascinating time, as many of the old rules that separate the races are breaking down and disappearing. She is in the first generation of the new South Africa.

Background: A colorful weaving by a rural artist.
Below: The Ndebele give these beaded dolls to new brides.

FOR YOUR INFORMATION: South Africa

Official Name: Republic of South Africa

Capitals: Pretoria, Cape Town, and Bloemfontein

History

The First Inhabitants: Prehistory to 1488

Archaeologists have determined that prehistoric human ancestors lived in South Africa almost two million years ago. We know about them only from fossil remains, such as the skull known as the "Taung Child." By the Middle Stone Age (40,000-9000 BC), South African cave dwellers were producing rock paintings and using stone tools such as hand axes, spearheads, knives, and scrapers.

By the Late Stone Age, 8,000 years ago, people called the San hunted and gathered in South Africa. About 2,000 years ago, some of the San bought sheep and cattle from tribes in the north and became herders. These herders became known as the Khoikhoi. Neither the San nor the Khoikhoi grew crops because they moved with the migration of animal herds.

Johannesburg, South Africa's largest city.

The rest of South Africa had very few people until about AD 1200, when many Bantu-speaking tribes from the north began to move southward to find better grazing and farming land. These migrants became the Zulu, Tsonga, Sotho, Swazi, Tswana, Venda, and Xhosa peoples. Soon, these well-organized tribes grew stronger and larger and forced the San and Khoikhoi from their land. By the time the first Europeans arrived in 1488, the eastern part of what is now South Africa was home to these newer tribes, while the San and Khoikhoi lived in the drier lands to the west.

European Settlement: 1488 to 1795

In 1488, the Portuguese explorer Bartholomeu Dias rounded the Cape of Good Hope while searching for a sea route to India. Ten years later, Vasco da Gama sailed by the same route all the way to India, stopping to trade with the Khoikhoi for fresh meat and supplies. Although many European ships later stopped in South Africa over the years, none stayed.

The first permanent European settlement began in 1652, when the Dutch sent 104 people to the Cape of Good Hope to start farming. These farms thrived and the Dutch colony grew bigger. Soon, the Dutch farms spread into the Khoikhoi lands to the north, forcing out the Khoikhoi. In addition, the Dutch raided the native villages, enslaving many of the Khoikhoi and San.

In 1688, the Catholic monarchy in France forced many Protestants to leave their country. Some of these Protestants, called Huguenots, came to South Africa and settled with the Dutch.

Because so few women lived in the early settlements (the first group of 104 had only four!), many of the Dutch men married San and Khoikhoi women. Most of their mixed-race children were known as the "Cape Coloured" people. Instead of living in the tribal communities of their mothers according to African tradition, many lived and worked with their fathers' people. Others separated into new tribes. Meanwhile, diseases brought by Europeans hit the San and Khoikhoi hard. Many died in a smallpox epidemic in 1713, and the rest re-treated north into the barren lands where they could keep their old way of life.

The Dutch, the Cape Coloured, and the French lived together for over two centuries, almost completely cut off from European influences. They developed their own language, called Afrikaans, and their own traditions and government. United by language, they became a separate people, almost like a new tribe, calling themselves "Afrikaners" (although the name later came to describe only those of white Dutch ancestry). But their differences in skin color and background prevailed; darker people were considered inferior legally and politically.

The Great Trek

In 1794, France attacked Holland. The Dutch king fled to England, which had sided with Holland against France. In South Africa, the British were afraid that the French navy would attack Cape Town. So, the next year, the British invaded and took over the Cape Colony.

Many Dutch settlers did not want to live under a British government that insisted on freeing its slaves, especially after British colonists began to arrive in 1820. They decided to move north into new and unsettled land in an area known as the Transvaal, a name that means "across the Vaal [River]." From 1834 to 1838, they and their families made the long, hard journey over the mountains, with their belongings packed into wagons. This migration became known as "the Great Trek," and the "Voortrekkers" compared themselves to the pioneers who settled in western North America at about the same time.

All this time, the Zulu had been growing stronger and more warlike. Under their leader, Shaka, they invaded the lands of other tribes and killed over a million people. This "kill or conquer" policy, called *mfecane*, left entire areas empty of inhabitants.

To defend themselves against the Zulu, some tribes joined together into a new tribal nation called the Ndebele and moved north into lands still held by the Khoikhoi. Unfortunately, the Voortrekkers, also known as Boers, were moving into the same lands as the Ndebele. Many fights broke out between them, but the Boers were determined to stay and make great farms out of the wild lands of the Transvaal. Both the Boers and the Ndebele hunted down and killed the Khoikhoi. After a battle in 1837, most of the Ndebele fled farther north, leaving the Boers in control of the Transvaal.

The Boer War

By the mid-1850s, South Africa had been carved into four separate colonies. In addition to Cape Colony in the west, the Boer farmers established the Orange Free State, the Colony of Natal, and the independent Republic of Transvaal in the east. The Boers were afraid that the British would try to take over the Transvaal and the Orange Free State as they had Cape Colony and, in 1843, Natal. The British, in turn, disliked the way the Boers raided native villages and enslaved children. Tensions between the Boers and the British were high.

Then, in 1867, diamonds were discovered near Kimberley, and in 1886, gold was found in the Transvaal. Europeans came to make their fortunes in the diamond and gold mines, and many blacks, who had been driven from their lands by the Zulu, came to work in the mines. Others came to earn money to pay the heavy taxes demanded by the Boers.

Attracted by this wealth, the British prime minister of the Cape Colony, Cecil Rhodes, made plans to seize the Boer territories and form one republic. But the Boers resented the British and resisted their attempts to govern South Africa. In 1899, war broke out. Over 450,000 British troops fought 80,000 Boers. The British put thousands of Boer women and children into prison camps, and 20,000 of them died. Unable to keep fighting, the Boers surrendered in 1902, and all of South Africa became part of the British Empire. In 1910, all four territories merged into one nation called the Union of South Africa.

The Law of Apartheid

From the beginning of the new nation, the Boers insisted on a firm policy of white rule. The British agreed to this in order to keep peace within the government. In 1912, the African National Congress, or ANC, was founded to fight for political rights and better treatment for black South Africans. But in 1948, the Nationalist party came to power and introduced a policy of racial segregation called "apartheid." Under apartheid, different races were to be kept completely apart. Areas called "homelands" were set aside for blacks, who lost their South African citizenship and were ordered to live in remote areas once occupied by their ancestors.

Despite persecution, whites, blacks, Coloureds, and Indians began working together to try to change the country's unjust laws. Chief Albert Luthuli won a Nobel Peace Prize in 1960 for organizing a nonviolent campaign for civil rights. That same year, the ANC was banned. Nelson Mandela, who organized an underground movement that blew up power plants and factories, was sentenced to life imprisonment in 1961. South Africa broke the last of its ties with Britain and became the Republic of South Africa at the same time.

During the 1970s and 1980s, demonstrations against apartheid often turned violent when protestors were attacked by police. Sometimes, people were arrested or killed without cause, setting off huge riots. Hundreds of people died from being shot by police or burned alive by rioters.

The violence of the protests brought South Africa's problems to the attention of the whole world. Other countries began to pressure the government to change its apartheid laws. Several countries, including the United States and Canada, restricted trade with South Africa, hoping that if South Africa couldn't buy or sell what it needed, it would do away with apartheid.

Foreign companies closed their offices and factories in South Africa, causing more than 60,000 black miners to lose their jobs. Many black leaders, including Gatsha Buthelezi, chief of the Zulu, opposed this international pressure because he believed that it hurt blacks more than whites. But others, such as Mandela and Archbishop Desmond Tutu, felt that pressure helped change the apartheid laws.

Recently, the situation in South Africa has been getting better. In 1980, hotels, libraries, and restaurants that had been closed to blacks opened to all people. In 1983, Indians and Coloureds were elected to Parliament. By 1986, most of the remaining apartheid laws were repealed. In 1987, the Natal province and the Zulu homeland merged under the leadership of Chief Buthelezi, the first black to be elected head of one of South Africa's four provinces. But blacks are still not allowed to vote in national elections or to live wherever they choose.

In 1989, the more moderate government of F. W. De Klerk was elected and changes came more quickly. Protest meetings and rallies were allowed, and open public discussion of racial problems began. In 1990, Mandela, leader of the ANC, was freed after nearly 28 years in prison. Despite these advances, many of the attitudes and frictions created by apartheid remain, including power struggles among black political groups. South Africa may be on the road to equality and justice, but much work and struggle yet remain.

Government

South Africa has a parliamentary system, in which the state president is chosen by 50 white, 25 Coloured, and 13 Indian members of Parliament. The president holds office for five years and appoints a cabinet to advise him. He has the power to veto laws, convene and dismiss Parliament, and declare war.

The constitution adopted in 1984 established three houses of Parliament: the House of Assembly for whites, the House of Representatives for Coloureds, and the House of Delegates for Indians. Laws that concern only one racial group are discussed and passed by its corresponding house, with the approval of the other two. Laws that affect the nation must be passed by all three houses. Voters aged 18 and over elect the members of the house of their own race.

Although they make up 74% of the population, blacks may not vote and have no representation in Parliament. This is because the government considers blacks to be citizens not of South Africa but of their "homeland." So blacks may only vote for their local "homeland" governments. Many South Africans now agree that they must find a way to bring blacks into the country's government and give fair representation to each tribal group. How they will do this is the major problem, since the smaller tribal groups fear the rule of the Zulu majority.

In addition to the national government, each of the country's four provinces — the Orange Free State, Transvaal, Natal, and Cape Province — have local councils. Each of these has a mayor and an elected executive committee made up of all the races that live in the province, including blacks. The "homelands" elect their own governments.

Courts are open to all people, regardless of race, but no jury system exists, and many accused people are jailed without trials. People may have a lawyer represent them, but only if they can pay the lawyer's fees. Those who cannot afford a lawyer must do without one. In the "homelands," blacks may choose to have civil cases heard by local chiefs and tribal elders who judge according to the traditions and customs of their people. But criminal cases and the cases of black city dwellers are tried in the white judicial system.

Currency

South Africa's monetary unit is called the *rand*, named for the area of the country where gold is mined. One rand equals 100 cents. The smallest bill is 2 rand and the largest in common use is 100 rand. There are 1-, 2-, 5-,10-, 20-, and 50-cent coins. They have pictures of South African wildlife and flowers.

South African currency.

Peoples and Languages

Few other nations on earth have such a wide variety of racial and tribal groups. Often, different groups of blacks may only communicate in one of the two white languages, English or Afrikaans, which are the official languages of South Africa.

Of South Africa's 37 million people, 74% are black, less than 14% are white, less than 9% are Coloured, and about 3% are Indian. But neither whites nor blacks are from a single ethnic background. Most blacks belong to one of nine distinct groups and most whites to one of four. What follows is a list of the main ethnic groups and their languages.

Afrikaners

About 60% of whites are descendants of the original Dutch settlers or those who have emigrated from Holland and Germany since. They speak Afrikaans, which is based on the Dutch language. Most of South Africa's farms are owned by Afrikaners.

British

Descendants of the original British settlers were joined by many more emigrants from the British Isles. They not only retained their English language and social customs, but brought with them British ideals, such as free speech.

Coloured (Mixed-Race)

Two groups form the Coloured population. The first group is descended from the children of Dutch men and Khoikhoi women. The second is descended from Malays brought from Asia by the Dutch East India Company in the 17th and 18th centuries. Most Coloureds have European customs and religions, and nearly all speak Afrikaans.

Indians

Indians make up about 3% of the population. When India and South Africa were British colonies, many Indians moved to South Africa, where they became prosperous merchants. They speak English, Hindi, and other Indian languages.

Zulu

The most numerous of South Africa's black groups, five million Zulu outnumber the next largest group by more than two to one. Zulu share a common language, and because their language is widespread, Zulu is understood by many other blacks as well. Over 50% live in the "homeland" of KwaZulu.

Xhosa

Over 2.5 million blacks are Xhosa, but unlike the Zulu, they do not share a common language. The Xhosa have many different dialects, or variations of their language, that may not be understood by other Xhosa.

Other Ethnic Groups

The Swazi, two groups of Sothos, the Tswanas, the Shangans, and others make up the rest of the population. The original San and Khoikhoi peoples have disappeared, except for a very few San who live in the far north. The San language, like the languages of some other African ethnic groups, uses a click sound. The click is written as "!" at the beginning of words such as !Kung (pronounced click-KUNG).

Land and Climate

South Africa covers the entire southern tip of the African continent. The sea surrounds the country on three sides. South Africa's neighbors to the north are Namibia, Botswana, Zimbabwe, and Mozambique. Two small, independent kingdoms, Swaziland and Lesotho, lie completely or mostly within its borders. South Africa also has land outside its main borders — Walvis Bay, a small piece of land carved out of Namibia, and two small islands near Antarctica.

South Africa covers an area of 471,445 square miles (1,221,042 sq km) and is somewhat smaller than the U.S. state of Alaska or the Canadian province of Quebec. For all its shoreline, it has few bays or good harbors, and no rivers suitable for boat traffic.

Most of the country's interior is a high, flat plateau, with an average elevation of 3,600 feet (1,100 m). This region, called a *thirstland*, is dry and desertlike. Vast, rolling grasslands called *bushveld* make up the other areas. The low areas between the foot of the plateau and the coasts have heavy rainfall and are covered with thick, green forests and millions of wildflowers.

Where the high and low areas meet is called an *escarpment*, a band of mountains and cliffs where the land drops off suddenly. It is easy to see why the first Europeans to see these mountains gave them names like Drakensberg (Dragon Mountain) and Giant's Castle. Rivers at the edge of the escarpment have carved out great canyons and steep gorges in the stone, often topped by lush forests.

In the north lies part of the great Kalahari Desert. The land there is so parched that people may see water flowing in the dry riverbeds only once or twice in their entire lifetimes.

While the Kalahari and the central plateau can be blistering hot in the summer and snow falls on the mountain summits in winter, most of the country is mild and pleasant year-round. Days are clear, sunny, and dry, and droughts are common. Even in normal seasons, rain is scarce and fields have to be irrigated to produce crops. The coast gets more rain.

Because South Africa is below the equator, its seasons are the opposite of those of the United States and Canada, with the warmest weather in December and January and the coldest in June and July. But only about 30°F (17°C) separates summer and winter temperatures, with even less variation along the coast.

South Africa has a rare variety of wild animal and plant life. Kruger National Park alone has more species of wildlife than are found in any other African reserve. Unlike other African countries, South Africa began to protect its game by the 1860s. While other countries allowed big-game hunters to kill too many animals, South Africa controlled hunting and dealt harshly with poachers.

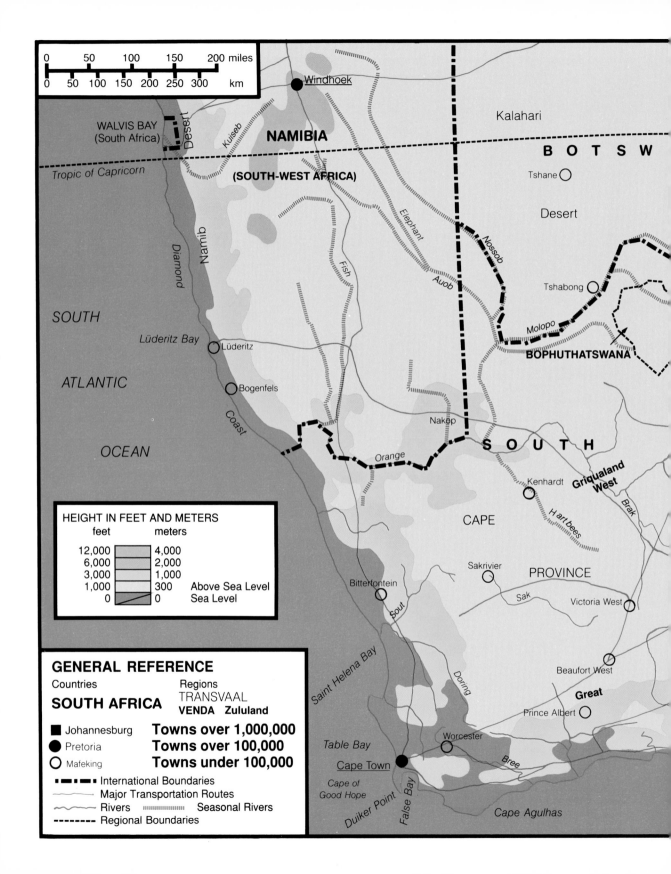

Scale:

0	50	100	150	200 miles

| 0 | 50 | 100 | 150 | 200 | 250 | 300 | km |

Windhoek

WALVIS BAY
(South Africa)

Desert

Kuiseb

NAMIBIA

Kalahari

Tshane ○

B O T S W

Tropic of Capricorn

(SOUTH-WEST AFRICA)

Desert

Diamond

Namib

Fish

Elephant

Auob

Nossob

SOUTH

Tshabong ○

Lüderitz Bay ○ Lüderitz

Molopo

BOPHUTHATSWANA

ATLANTIC

○ Bogenfels

Coast

OCEAN

Nakop

Orange

S O U T H

Kenhardt ○

Griqualand West

HEIGHT IN FEET AND METERS

feet	meters	
12,000	4,000	
6,000	2,000	
3,000	1,000	
1,000	300	Above Sea Level
0	0	Sea Level

H art bees

Brak

CAPE

Sakrivier ○

PROVINCE

Bitterfontein ○

Sout

Sak

Victoria West ○

Saint Helena Bay

Doring

Beaufort West ○

GENERAL REFERENCE

Countries

SOUTH AFRICA

Regions
TRANSVAAL
VENDA Zululand

■ Johannesburg **Towns over 1,000,000**

● Pretoria **Towns over 100,000**

○ Mafeking **Towns under 100,000**

▪▬▪▬ International Boundaries

—— Major Transportation Routes

〜〜 Rivers ‧‧‧‧‧‧‧ Seasonal Rivers

- - - - Regional Boundaries

Great

Prince Albert ○

Table Bay

Worcester ○

Cape Town ●

*Cape of
Good Hope*

Bree

Duiker Point

False Bay

Cape Agulhas

SOUTH AFRICA — Political and Physical

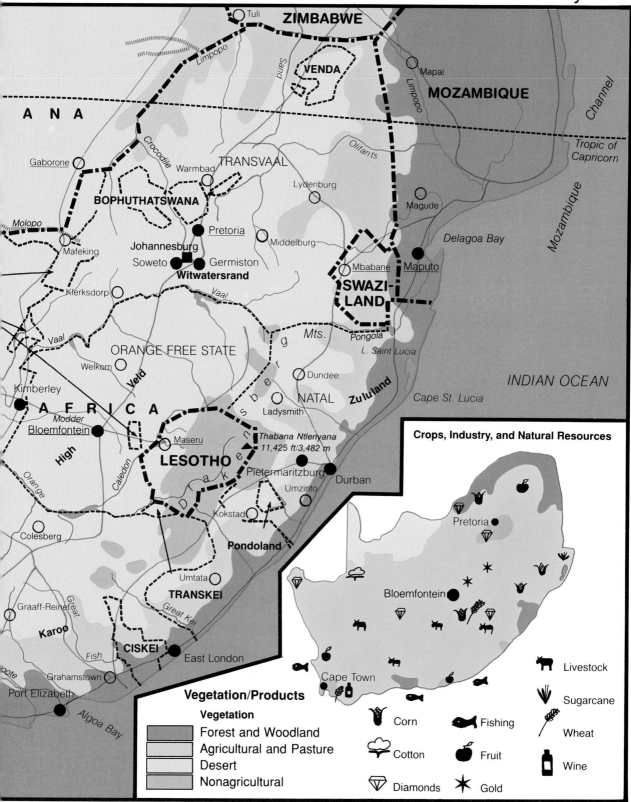

ZIMBABWE
Tuli
Limpopo
Sand
VENDA
Mapai
MOZAMBIQUE
Limpopo
Channel
Olifants
Tropic of Capricorn
A N A
Gaborone
Crocodile
TRANSVAAL
Warmbad
Lydenburg
Magude
Delagoa Bay
Mozambique
Molopo
Pretoria
Middelburg
Mbabane
Maputo
Mafeking
Johannesburg
Soweto
Germiston
Witwatersrand
SWAZI-LAND
Klerksdorp
Vaal
Pongola
L. Saint Lucia
BOPHUTHATSWANA
g
Mts.
Vaal
ORANGE FREE STATE
Welkom
Veld
Dundee
NATAL
Zululand
INDIAN OCEAN
Cape St. Lucia
Kimberley
A F R I C A
Ladysmith
Modder
Bloemfontein
Maseru
Thabana Ntlenyana
11,425 ft/3,482 m
High
LESOTHO
Pietermaritzburg
Durban
Caledon
Umzinto
Orange
Kokstad
Colesberg
Pondoland
Umtata
TRANSKEI
Graaff-Reinet
Great
Great Kei
Karoo
CISKEI
Fish
East London
Grahamstown
Port Elizabeth
Algoa Bay

Crops, Industry, and Natural Resources

Pretoria
Bloemfontein
Cape Town

Vegetation/Products

Vegetation
Forest and Woodland
Agricultural and Pasture
Desert
Nonagricultural

Corn
Cotton
Diamonds
Fishing
Fruit
Gold

Livestock
Sugarcane
Wheat
Wine

Industry and Natural Resources

Despite its dry climate and poor soil, and with only 12% of its land under cultivation, South Africa grows more food on its farms than any other African nation. Not only do these farms feed South Africans, but long lines of trucks cross its borders every day to bring corn, milk, eggs, meat, and fruit to neighboring countries, without which many would starve.

Corn is the major crop and is the basic food of most rural blacks. Wheat, sugar, beans, and fruit are also major crops. Farmers raise cattle for meat, hides, and dairy foods and sheep for both meat and wool. South Africa's wool production is the sixth largest in the world.

South Africa's greatest riches lie buried deep beneath its poor soil. Its mines produce more gold than does any other country in the world. South Africa is also the world's largest exporter of minerals, with ample supplies of diamonds, platinum, chromium, coal, uranium, iron ore, and nickel. All but about 15% of this is sold to other countries. Mineral mining employs over 730,000 workers, most of them blacks.

For many years, South Africa exported minerals and imported most of its manufactured goods. But since the 1960s, it has steadily increased its manufacturing, especially after foreign countries refused to trade with it and imported goods became scarce. Products ranging from processed foods and clothing to chemicals and heavy equipment are now produced in South Africa.

Arts and Culture

South Africa's diverse peoples give it a rich artistic heritage. Traditional black culture rings with song, drama, dance, and stories told around village fires. Many of these art forms record events, tell stories, or pass traditions from one generation to the next. Tribal arts, ranging from intricate beadwork and basket making to unusual stone and wood sculpture, reflect the varied ethnic identities of the black peoples.

"Zulu love letters" are beaded necklaces that are given by girls to their boyfriends.

Some artists find inspiration in South Africa's social structure. The author Alan

Paton and playwright Athol Fugard have created their characters and plots out of the injustices of racial discrimination. Black playwrights Gibson Kente and Sam Mhangwani create plays using everyday life as a theme.

In the performing arts, people of all races have been working together for many years. At Windybrow, a restored mansion from the early days of Johannesburg, performing arts groups have built a new theater where blacks and whites work side by side as managers, directors, performers, and volunteers, and enjoy watching performances together.

Most of South Africa's tribal peoples share the art of creating beautiful decorations from beads. Some use beadwork for clothing, others decorate ceremonial dolls, and others make jewelry. The Zulu use beads as a way of communicating. "Zulu love letters" use beads in simple patterns that convey a message. Colors can mean different things in different villages, but white, green, and red beads usually mean love; black, loneliness; yellow, home; and pink, a promise.

Religion

Since Europeans first began coming to South Africa, missionaries from many religions have taught their beliefs to the local people. As a result, both blacks and whites practice some of the same religions. More than 75% are Christian, with the largest churches being the Dutch Reformed, Roman Catholic, Anglican, and Methodist. A small Jewish community also exists. Most Asians are Hindus, but some are Muslims and a few are Christians.

Traditional tribal religions are still very important to rural blacks. Most are based on a belief in one supreme being and ancestor worship, in which the spirits of dead family members participate in everyday life. Family ties are very important, since the ancestors are believed to look after their own family members. Priests also play a vital part in daily village life, often settling arguments.

Education

Historically, the South African government has spent much more money on educating white children than black children. South Africa tries to teach all of its children the languages spoken in their homes. But because of a shortage of trained teachers in native languages, most black South African children either only get a few years of schooling or else are taught in English or Afrikaans. Today, about 80% of black children attend school. Despite South Africa's problems in teaching its many peoples, both blacks and whites have the highest literacy rate in all of Africa.

Because of the variety of languages, children of different ethnic groups attend different schools. Even British and Afrikaner students often go to different schools, so the separation is not a strictly racial one.

Most students attend public schools, and about 5% attend private schools run by churches. Schooling lasts 12 years and is divided into three stages: four years of lower primary school, three years of higher primary school, and five years of high school.

The government has established colleges and universities for the different races. After 12 years of school, students "sit for matriculation," taking examinations for placement in colleges, universities, and technical schools.

Sports and Recreation

The climate is nearly perfect for outdoor sports all year round, and people of all races participate in individual and team sports regularly. Soccer is the most popular street sport. Soweto alone has over 100 soccer fields, not counting the parks, playgrounds, streets, and empty lots where neighborhood boys gather to play. Day or night, a soccer game is almost always going on.

Among whites, rugby is the most popular sport and a compulsory activity for boys in many schools. The national team, the Springboks, is one of the best in the world. Cricket is another popular sport.

A program called Trimsa (Trim South Africa) started in 1979 to encourage people of all ages to become fit and active. It sponsors sports courses and competitions and builds facilities for sports and exercise. Trimsa offers family runs, Trim-Gyms, bicycle trips, and Trim-Parks with walking and running trails.

Girls take physical education in school, but girls and women do not usually take part in competitive team or street sports.

Pretoria, Bloemfontein, and Cape Town

When the Union of South Africa was formed, each of its four provinces was afraid that a city in one of the other provinces would be chosen as the nation's capital and become more powerful than the rest. The only answer seemed to be to put each branch of the government in a different city, and that's why South Africa has three capitals. Pretoria, a small, modern city just north of Johannesburg, is where the state president and administrative offices are.

Bloemfontein, which means "fountain of flowers" in Afrikaans, grew into the judicial capital from a tiny frontier outpost. Bloemfontein is in the center of the country, and many people think that the other two branches of the government should move there so that the country would have one capital city.

Beautiful Cape Town is the legislative capital, where Parliament meets. The original Company Garden of the Dutch East India Company still cuts a green path through the center of Cape Town. Above the city towers Table Mountain, and at its feet opens a wide bay to the Atlantic Ocean.

South Africans in North America

Before 1976, as few as 40 South Africans moved to the United States and Canada each year. That number increased in the late 1970s to nearly 1,000 a year, when some whites began to fear racial unrest. But in recent years, immigration has dropped to about 850 annually.

Glossary of Useful South African Terms

Tswana
dumela (doo-MEH-lah) ....hello
go siame (goh see-AH-may) ....that is fine

Zulu
ngiyabonga (en-gee-yah-BOH-gah) ....thank you
sakubona (sah-koo-BOH-nah) ....hello

Afrikaans
asseblief (AHS-ehb-leef) ....please
dankie (DAHN-kee) ....thank you

More Books about South Africa

Journey to Jo'burg: A South African Story. Naidoo (Harper Junior Books)
South Africa. Lawson (Franklin Watts)
We Live in South Africa. Kristensen (Franklin Watts)

Things to Do — Research Projects

South Africa is one of the richest yet one of the most troubled nations in the world. Its apartheid policies have caused unrest at home and condemnation abroad. As South Africa struggles to change to a system of racial equality, its leaders try to satisfy the demands of both whites and blacks.

As you study South Africa, remember the importance of having up-to-date facts. Listed below are two reference books that will tell you where to find the latest articles on South Africa. As you read, try to compare different accounts of the same events to get a complete picture of what is really happening.

Readers' Guide to Periodical Literature
Children's Magazine Guide

1. Under the laws of apartheid, what rights do whites have that other South Africans do not? In what ways are blacks and whites separated? Find out what blacks and whites are doing to change the laws.

2. Who are the most prominent black leaders in South Africa? What have they done on behalf of the struggle for racial equality and justice?

More Things to Do — Activities

1. Art in South Africa ranges from the cave paintings of the San to Zulu bead-work and Ndebele murals. Find pictures of these in books on African art. Create your own paintings or jewelry in these styles and decorate your schoolroom with them.

2. If you would like a pen pal from South Africa, write to one of these organizations:

   International Pen Friends
   P.O. Box 290065
   Brooklyn, NY 11229

   Worldwide Pen Friends
   P.O. Box 39097
   Downey, CA 90241

   When you write, be sure to tell them which country you want your pen pal to be from, and always include your name, address, and age.

Tumi waves good-bye from the steps of her school.

Index